The Weary World Rejoices

THE WEARY WORLD REJOICES

Steve Fellner

MARSH HAWK PRESS

EAST ROCKAWAY, NY • 2011

11 12 13 14 15 • 7 6 5 4 3 2 1   FIRST EDITION

Marsh Hawk Press books are published by Poetry Mailing List, Inc.,
a not-for-profit corporation under section 501 (c) 3
United States Internal Revenue Code.

Cover and interior design by Claudia Carlson.
The text is set in Fairfield and display in Neutra.

Library of Congress Cataloging-in-Publication Data

Fellner, Steve.
  The weary world rejoices / Steve Fellner.
    p. cm.
  ISBN-13: 978-0-9846353-0-6 (pbk.)
  ISBN-10: 0-9846353-0-0 (pbk.)
  I. Title.
  PS3606.E3885W43 2011
  811'.6--dc22

              2011012817

Marsh Hawk Press
P.O. Box 206, East Rockaway, N.Y. 11518-0206
www.marshhawkpress.org

for the young gay men
who never found a way

Acknowledgements

The author gratefully wishes to acknowledge the editors who have selected the following poems to be included in their magazines. *Barn Owl Review:* "Think of a Knock as Something Other than Simple, Useless Etiquette" • *Huffington Post:* "Three Blocks from the Mosque" • *No Tell Motel:* "Shoelaces," "Ode to Matthew Shepard," "Ode to Judy Shepard," "Ode to My Lover," "Upon Imagining the Field where Matthew Shepard was Murdered" • *OCHO:* "Ode to Agoraphobia" • *Sugar House Review:* "Doctor's Note," "Secret Ingredients" • *TriQuarterly:* "I am Known as Walt Whitman," "Russia is Big and so is China" • *Web Del Sol:* "Ode to Crystal Meth."

"Doctor's Note," "Secret Ingredients," and "Get-Away" are collaborative prose poems. They were written with Phil E. Young.

He thanks editors David Kirby and Barbara Hamby for reprinting "Russia Is Big and So Is China" in their anthology *Seriously Funny: Poems about Love, Death, Religion, Art, Politics, Sex, and Everything Else* from University of Georgia Press.

He thanks all his friends and family who helped him through. You know who you are.

For their critical input on the manuscript, he thanks Zia Isola, Samantha Ruckman, Nicole Walker, Anne Panning, Lindsey Brown, Eliot Khalil Wilson, Sophia Kartsonis, and Sarah Cedeño. He thanks Sandy McIntosh and Ira Sadoff for their strong advice and poetic wisdom. He thanks Rebecca Livingston for publishing some of his Matthew Shepard poems. It gave him the faith to continue writing this book. He thanks Claudia Carlson for her patience, talent.

And, of course, he thanks his partner Phil E. Young who gave him the title of this book (for a small fee), endless advice, and for being the most talented, most gentle, cutest man he knows.

TABLE OF CONTENTS

I

II

III

I

GLOBALIZATION

Watch out Harlem
Globetrotters! Spinning that ball
on your finger doesn't wow me now.
Not too much anyway. Sixth grade,
geography class. We needed
to memorize the world.
I started with Antarctica,
then Zimbabwe. I've never liked
middles. Typical homosexual:
depressed, no good
at sports. The whirl of a globe
fascinated me. Dizziness
was a sign of vitality. Who
doesn't need to feel untethered
from the world once in a while?
I was a straight A student. Gay
overachiever. Much to my shame,
I still can only remember one thing:
the correct answers.
Everything is either true or false.
That's how I survived my mother.
She collected miniature doll houses;
myself, globes, all different sizes and colors.
"Step back," she said. Awe:
the sight of a dozen globes rotating one after another.
There you have it! Things always keep
on moving. Even if family can only stay put.
This is our secret: my mother shrunk
to the size of my thumb. Her demand:
an add-on and garage
to the unoccupied doll house.
Her snore was a welcome earthquake.
A goodbye gift: a snowglobe.
Making a wish, I shook it so hard
it broke. The snow no longer churned.
All I had were the chips, a trick
gone wrong, a hoop with no hole.

"RUSSIA IS BIG AND SO IS CHINA"

Overheard statement from President Bush
at summit with Chinese President Hu Jintao.

Monopoly is fun and so is strip poker.
The weather is nice and so is this iced tea.
Porcupine quills are sharp and so is that pair of scissors. Be careful, OK?
The baby across the aisle from you is loud and so is some rap music.
The GED was hard and so was bungee jumping.
Pink is a color and so is salmon. Salmon is also a fish.
Bruce Willis is still hot and so is Kurt Cobain, though he's dead.
Stoplights are annoying and so are brussels sprouts.
Vitamin C is good for you and so is exercise.
I could stand to lose ten pounds and so could you.
I am lazy and you don't have anywhere else to be.
North Korea is fidgety and so is my little sister. No Ritalin for her.
I am horny and so are most of my dumb friends.
Seven is more than three and so is eight.
The news is strange and so is my hairdresser.
Model airplanes are frustrating and so are summits.
Poisoned Halloween candy is creepy and so is anthrax.
Used dental floss is icky and so are missiles.
Nuclear weapons are large and so is my penis.
Metaphors are always obvious and so is common sense.
Wisdom is cheap and so is bus fare.
Solar energy is easy and so is my ex-boyfriend Nick.
Armageddon is a bummer and so is Picasso.

CLOUDS

Clouds have no strategy. Or so one thinks. They are benign.
Kind things. They block the sunlight from hitting us all day long.
You can only have so much sunlight. So much direct address from up above.
God and sunlight can only hit you so many times.
Before you need something like a cloud to protect you. You look up
At the sky and a cloud becomes whatever you want.
My mother always took us to the park to look up at the sky.
The clouds became objects, animals, worlds
We never would have thought to see. It was a strategy.
A strategy to get us through the days.
To make the time with her seem almost bearable.
She often forgot her own moves, failing to look up,
Letting other things hit her. Like sadness. Like despair.
Like madness. Things that you can't control.
You can only be hit by those things so many times
Before you look up. Or else all you become is strategy.
And that's no good. No good at all if you want sunlight
To pour through God and for Him to be as benign as His own cloud.

St. Sebastian

How many St. Sebastian statues
can I give as coming out gifts?
My life: cheap porcelain,
phony exclamations

of surprise. At The Fruit Loop,
I see my Catholic neighbor,
two cocks in his mouth. Meanwhile
a deer rubs his nose against kudzu.

High school gym class: teacher,
Vietnam vet, PTSD. "Someone
is hitting me from the bleachers
with invisible arrows." I don't

know what it's like to be shot
in the head. I don't know
what it's like to be tied
to a post. Once I visited

a friend in the hospital.
He took my face in his hands.
"If God made you beautiful,
you'd be in the other bed."

THE END OF THE WORLD

Some people volunteered to make the world lighter. It wasn't like the old days
when you put everybody's name in a hat. Someone pulled

out a slip of paper. The slip of paper was heavy. The hat was heavy.
Once the names of the people broke through the bottom of the hat. People died

without even knowing it. *That's how it's going to be when it's the end
of the world,* my friend said. I told him I didn't read science fiction books.

I tore out pages. I wrote the names of friends who I wanted to die before me.
I made a lot of friends back then. Too many countries made too many enemies.

So much bloodshed. No matter where you stood you could hear the sound
of people dying. To make myself feel better, I bought a hat.

I was a bit of a dandy. Everyone was thinking about what to do
with the dead bodies. No one told me how good the hat looked on me.

One night my hat grew to epic proportions. I didn't know how
it happened. But it did. It became as large as your average Midwestern state.

People all over the world traveled to pile dead bodies alongside the brim.
Things became crowded pretty quick. If I stayed outside long enough,

I would see helicopters circling around the hat's crown,
preparing to drop bodies into an unoccupied space. I tried my best

to direct the traffic. No one listened to me. It was like a science fiction
movie. Foreign people doing odd things, vehicles colliding, dead bodies

littering the ground. I wrote the names of the dead on slips of paper.
One day I asked myself, *Is my hat a magic hat?* I climbed on top

of the dead bodies and peered into the darkness to see what was there.
The air felt light. I shouted a little. Not too loud. I didn't want to be

disrespectful. There were dead bodies all around me. I was careful not to fall into
the darkness. I dropped the slips of paper into the hat. I couldn't hear

any noise. If I had had any friends who were still alive, I would have sent them into the hat to find what was there. Wouldn't the end of the world

involve a tip of the hat? Feel like some sort of magic trick?
Wouldn't my friends come back from the dead? I was so light

I began to float. I looked down at the dead bodies, all slaughtered,
like in a science-fiction movie. I couldn't tell if the wars had stopped.

There were lame explosions here and there. Some screaming. Then
it dawned on me. I no longer had a hat to put on the top of my head.

ODE TO CRYSTAL METH

I have never thanked you
for taking away my sleep.
My dreams. I am so uncreative
my dreams are not worth
sharing. Childhood images undeserving
of a poem. Bedroom door refusing
to remain locked, severed hands
tickling me, kisses as hot
as a furnace, leaving scars
that only specialists beg to behold.
I am too weak to dream
in metaphor. Appreciate me
for working so hard
to be a victim.

ODE TO MISS PIGGY

The first time I made love,
I heard your karate chops
swishing the air,

punctuating my head
hitting the headboard.
His punches made me feel

I was sailing
through the air. Towards
something like outer space.

"Kermit's a pussy," I said.
He slapped me
as hard as he did his own kids:

hard. No doubt
their reddened asses
smarted when they sat

in front of the TV,
watching your primetime show.
We made sure the volume

was turned up high.
"Pig bottom," he said. "Lick
it up." O dear Miss Piggy,

don't think less
of me. You always kept your dignity.
I was an oinker. OINKOINKOINK!

It still feels so good
twenty-three years later,
fat, middle-aged, with a kid

not my own. I forced my partner
to buy *The Special Edition Muppet Show
Series One DVD.*

604 minutes of you. "See,"
I say to his kid, cheering
whenever you burst

onto the screen. "She's a fem-
inist," I add. He looks at me
like the asshole I am.

These days missionary sex
feels like a giant leap
for mankind. Don't forgive me

for transforming into a sad
spacecraft that longs to leave
Earth to find something divine

like a pair of your furry ears.

Doctor's Note

written in collaboration with Phil E. Young

His doctor told him that he was allergic to music. This explained the sudden rashes at the Scottish bagpipe festival, the nosebleeds at the high school chorus recital of Carmina Burana, the deep red welts that appeared halfway through a set by the band Sparklehorse at the 40 Watt club. But the incident that finally caused him to go to the doctor was when he joined his wife and his mother in singing "Happy Birthday to You" to his newborn daughter. Once he joined the chorus, he started to have a seizure so severe that everyone froze until his wife called an ambulance and his mother knelt next to him, doing her best to make sure he didn't bite his own tongue. She began to softly hum what she thought was an old Portuguese lullaby, partially to soothe him but mostly to calm her own nerves. It proved to be a terrible mistake. "Oh meu bebê na floresta/ Meu bebê precioso na floresta/ Meu pequeno na sombra/ Na sombra da floresta." He vomited blood. That incident seemed like nothing now, nothing compared to his anxiety in protecting himself from this affliction. The doctor tried to stifle his laughter when he asked if there was a shot or a pill he could take for this sort of thing. "What do I do, doc...what do I do for a life without music?" The doctor shook his head. "With every allergy there is some synthetic. Some miraculous substitution. For those who cannot smell flowers without their eye ducts swelling shut... ." He opened a drawer, pulled out an aerosol can, sprayed the air. "Voila! The synthetic rose. Inhale! Safe, fake, and nothing like the real thing. But, at the same time, just enough." The doctor rose, obviously eager to bring this meeting to an end. "You will find enough to pretend. Songs without music, stories without cadence, poems without rhythm, beat, or open throat. Great humanitarian committees are working in droves to produce such fabrications as we speak. In blue ribbon batches, with only a minimal application fee. I understand there's a whole cottage industry..." And with that, the doctor pushed the man out the door, to the waiting room, and in front of the receptionist, who, with probity, produced the bill. "But, I don't..." began the man, and then realized he had nothing to say. At least the doctor was kind enough to simply shake his head and then make a call to the management of the office building, asking if the elevator music could be shut off until the patient made it safely outside, where no birds ever seemed to be around, singing unnecessarily.

ODE TO AGORAPHOBIA

after Catullus

I am happy you kept my lover trapped
in his house, stuck
in front of the television, reluctant
to open the door for anyone
except the cable repairman. That was the best
gift for me when I deserted my beloved,
thinking I needed to leave
our own tiny space, choosing lovers
who slept outdoors, all of us afraid
we were going to miss out
on something. Now I am
back. Don't let anyone
accuse you of being selfish. There isn't much
on this planet you can't see
on the back of a postcard. Even so, I am full
of so much doubt that when I wake up
I always run onto our porch to make sure
the universe is still there. I go
for long walks alone. The birds mimic
the way I drag my heels. I am relieved
that my beloved never wants me
to leave. From the window, he watches me
march away. He presses his forehead
against the glass. For a moment, my body resides
inside the circle of his eye.

THE BURNING

A barn in Morgan County, Ohio was targeted by an arsonist.
After someone spray painted "fags are freaks" on the side of a
fence surrounding a barn, it was torched. — WHZ News

Eight horses died in a fire. But who's counting?
    Let me tell you a secret. I was always afraid
that those horses would stop running, their manes
    streaming in the winds, their hooves hitting

the ground with the speed of something
    like fire. Some say the man who owned the barn
looked like a horse. Others say the horse looked
    like the man. All I remember: looking at the barn,

seeing a man who looked at his horses with love,
    the same way I looked at him
through my bedroom window. I can't remember if I wanted
    him to see me or not. Have you ever touched

the ears of a horse when they're back flat against her
    neck, her white eyes exposed, angry as fire?
I saw the men who burned the barn. Here's a question:
    Did the men who burned the barn love the horses?

Were they, too, afraid that the horses would stop
    galloping and grazing in the meadows of grass?
The men seemed to admire the grass. It took a beating well.
    Sometimes when I saw the horses race

so fast over the grass, I thought it would catch on fire.
    I never loved fire. That's why I sat in my room,
looking through my window. That's why I never called
    anyone to put the fire out.

Was I the one who lit the fire, hoping
    that it would burn itself out?
I never possessed a match, never bought
    any gasoline. All I know: The fire burned and burned.

I am Known as Walt Whitman

To the gay men who spend their Friday nights lurking in the cyber chatroom,
I am known as Walt Whitman. My alias. My secret identity. My better half.
Somewhere in that claim a stupid joke can be found. Don't expect me

to discover it. I'm too busy online looking for the man who offered my
boyfriend his first taste of crystal meth. It got him so messed up he couldn't stop
meeting men off the Internet, and then begging them to stay

after they had their release. Of course, they always left. Bored,
he did other risky things like having sex in a bathroom stall at WalMart
where he was arrested for indecent exposure.

(Somewhere on those tiles there is a trace of him.)
He lost his job as a minimum wage earning bagboy at Wegman's,
causing him to avoid the grocery story altogether, the only one in town.

Crystal kidnaps your hunger anyway. His appetite resurfaced elsewhere.
Like in orgies where condoms were thought of as unnecessary ornaments.
(Somewhere in my voice, useless empathy can be found.) He contracted HIV.

I broke up with him because I didn't want to take care of someone
who was going to die in such an uninspired way. Somewhere in this narrative
there may be a shred of logic to be found. O, my dumb dead boyfriend,

you are my expired muse. Because I know you gave so kindly to strangers,
I imagine your hole as raw as the material for this poem.
Bloody and needy and lovely. Somewhere in your flesh I had wished

to find a reason to forgive you. Somewhere in your grave I will find
the redemption I'll need for hating you. Somewhere in another poem I will
find the strength to tell this story without invoking the name of Walt Whitman.

But now I need him. I need that dead homosexual to find a way
into my prayer for you. I can't let this be a poem about me and you.
It needs to be something larger. Something

that moves our words beyond a story of drugs,
a memoir of lonely people, a poem of catharsis.
Are you listening from the heavens, my worthless love?

II

SEVEN SECONDS

out of the womb
        And—boom!—
I see a portrait of myself:
bulging forehead, pug nose, over-
        sized arms. My mother is a caricature
artist. I look like the rough draft
of a Jim Henson Muppet
        someone ditched. I survey
all the stuffed animals awaiting my touch and think,
is everyone always so goddamned literal?
        Junior high,
school photographer receives note
from my mother: *Don't let him smile.*
        He looks better
blank. She has a point.
Dozen years later, I am all
        special effect
from bad horror film: blood-
shot eyes from drinking, ghost
        white skin from hiding
from sunlight, stitches
in forehead from banging head
        against walls
of holding rooms in psych ERs.
My mother will not let quacks
        sketch my problems
on drab notepads. Off she goes
to paint the landscape of my brain:
        My synapses like knotted
tree branches, serotonin
as low as flying birds, thoughts
        as dirty as a wounded
sky. Skip ahead a dozen years.
"I don't believe in God
        or metaphor,"
my mother says, sick, feeble.
"A splotch
        is a splotch is a splotch."

THINK OF A KNOCK AS
SOMETHING OTHER THAN SIMPLE,
USELESS ETIQUETTE

*"The Constitution does not require the government to forfeit
evidence gathered through illegal 'no knock' searches, the
Supreme Court ruled yesterday, in a far-reaching ruling that
could encourage police with search warrants to conduct
more aggressive raids."* – The Washington Post

Think of a knock as nothing less
than a way of life. Think of a knock as a tiny

exclamation from God himself. How else can He say,
"Here I am. Prepare for my arrival" without scaring someone?

Think of a knock as the most compressed of songs, one gracious enough to know
it cannot last forever, one humble enough to realize all notes sound

pretty much the same. Think of a knock as salvation
from all the other painful noise in the world: the uninspired

cry of bad childhoods, the rote explosions of dangerous weather,
the endless murmur of lame newscasters, the gross burps

of empty presidential promises. Think of a knock as a set-up
for a joke: *Knock knock. Who's there? Justin. Justin*

who? Just in time for another joke. In fact, here it is: The death
of a knock is the death of a world where one can find refuge

in dumb, undemanding sound. The words *I love you* cannot offer
what a knock does. Once I was ditched by my beloved.

He did not come back for months. Friends told me stories of how they made him
leave their place after they cooked him dinner, let him raid

their liquor cabinets. "He'll be back," they said.
"Does he really have anywhere else to go?" No

phone call from him, not even a hang-up. Then
there was a knock. For once, everything was perfect

until the words began. No one translates a knock
into meaning. No one asks a knock to be anything more

than the sound of skin and bone against wood, bereft
of an echo, thankful to be lost in a space

you should no longer dare to enter.

ELEGY

It's just a jump to left. And then
a step to the right. O Rocky
Balboa! Please have mercy
on someone who has only four toes.
I've never been able to find
my way around a ring without
a series of knockout punches
to my face. When I see
my best friend on the street
she looks as if she's walking
under water. All distorted wave
and dumb current. Once a young punk
pointed to my shoes, "Look
at that guy. He must be a fag.
He wears Birkenstocks."
What is a gay man to do?
Thirty-six years old, afraid
to let even the skin
on my feet breathe.
For a queer, I've never been a very good dresser.
I can still remember my first pair
of Doc Martin knock-offs.
They were half a size too small.
I squished my feet into them anyway.
The shoes finally fell apart
a few weeks ago. I thought it
would be cute to throw
a little funeral for them. I didn't.

DIAGNOSIS

A diagnosis is a wish. My sick and tired mother
Never realized when she went to doctor
After doctor that she was doing what she did for us
When we were young: taking us to a fountain
In the middle of the shopping mall and giving
Us pennies to feed the noisy water. The water
Was so loud back then. I can still hear it if I am alone
At night, suffering from insomnia. The water is still
Loud, I imagine, as the young children have replaced
Me and have fewer pennies to give the water. O generous
Water, how hard you tried to drown out the hopeless
Stares of the young! We are made up of water. So
Much so, I do not know why my mother
Thinks her body is poisoned, why
She goes to doctor after doctor, wishing that someone
Would hear her pain, give her a diagnosis. She can't sleep. No
Longer does she race out the door to take someone to the fountain
In the shopping mall. I try to bring the fountain
To her. The water is too loud and slips right through
My fingers. A lot like a wish. A lot like a diagnosis.
But I try to carry the fountain to her. It hurts my back.
Now my back always hurts. I wonder if the water
Was in pain, the way it seemed to burble and gurgle
The more we went to visit. The more you visit,
The more pain, I suppose. The more you get carried
Away from the fountain. The fountain doesn't move,
No matter how much you try to pick it up. Don't jump
Into the water. You'll hurt yourself and then
Someone else will have to throw pennies
Into the fountain to save you.

ODE TO MY FRIEND
WHO RECENTLY WON A PRESTIGIOUS POETRY BOOK CONTEST

after Catullus

We've been friends so long
I forgot I had reasons to despise you.
Your inability to keep love in your life
is my only proof that I may be better

with words than you. I know how to say
I love you in a way that matters
to someone else. Your book was selected
by a poet whose name will be forgotten

tomorrow. Her poems rewrite myths
in a way only a mortal could love.
She offers the stories of female gods
happy endings. As she did with you.

Something I know you will destroy
with the precision of one of your inspired
line breaks. Your lover put your baby
picture on his book cover. After he broke

up with you. After I begged you
to go back to your husband. After
his female student dedicated her book to him.
We wasted our time reading

your lover's poems, trying to figure out
if he'd take you back. All we knew
was life doesn't imitate art. But
the acknowledgements page does say something

about love. Your lover listed you
third. Behind two other women
who were younger and prettier than you.
But who cares about either of those men?

Now you have a book. You will win even more
prizes and readings and the love of men
who bore you. Bookless, hopeless,
I will sit at home with my beloved, thinking of you

reading your poems
to the hum of your air conditioner, waiting
for the phone to ring. It will be
me congratulating you, secretly wanting

to tell you your life is now worth living
only as material for my poems.

Ode to the Gay Man Who Claimed in His On-Line Personal That He Wasn't "Into Mind Games"

What else is there other than mind games? What else is there
in this world except gay men who are either bored or dead?
My boyfriend was bored. Now he's dead. I couldn't tell you the difference

between the two. He stopped talking long before he died.
Thank God, he was sick and lost his voice. He had an excuse.
I have no excuse for refusing to utter his name

unless I'm pretending to be him. As I do on Friday nights when I post
his picture on the Internet and his name becomes mine and I repeat the
promises he made me to someone else. This is the truth:

He had the body other men would die for. That's what he said in his personal.
Here's another truth: Men die of disappointment when they see
my body. Once a man visited me thinking I was my boyfriend. And alive.

When he knocked on the door, I answered, and then he stared at me
like I should have been someone else. He looked so disappointed.
"Don't be a baby," I wanted to say. "I go through that every day."

I expected him to excuse himself, say that he left his phone in the car
or that his family restaurant was burning down and he did feel obligated,
after all, to leave and clean up the ashes. But instead

he did something much worse. He said, "Not what I expected.
But good enough." Good enough. How can one man ever be good enough?
How can one mind, especially when it's your own,

ever be good enough? The mind is not a good enough playground
when the outside world has disappeared and been replaced by the thunder
of endless keystrokes. Another time: I met another man who expected to meet

my dead lover. I opened the door and then the man said, "I confess. I'm sorry.
Your boyfriend and I did have an affair." I never told him he died. How can
you tell someone that the only reason you want him to apologize is to hear

the sound of someone's voice? He did say sorry in the only way he could:
he made love to a body as lifeless and still as the corpse
I pretended I wanted to be. One last memory, one final game: Weeks ago,

I encountered a man I could have loved. For hours, we talked
about the unnecessary: our dreams we forgot, our desires we lost.
He offered me his picture several times. I didn't want to see his photo

before we met. He was offering me hope. That horrible thing.
But then he sent it anyway. It was a photo of my dead boyfriend, looking
happy, the same picture I had sent to countless men. He hadn't even bothered

to disguise the fact that he had forwarded the photo to dozens of others.
My dead boyfriend was alive
in everybody's inbox, ignorant, as he always was, that he could be wiped out

by someone else's innocent gesture.

ODE TO JAMES SCHUYLER

I cruise
your poems for the names
of pharmaceuticals.

Entertaining to think I might
be on the same stuff
as my idol.

Nowhere do I see
a diagnosis though.
Too many flowers blocking

the view. Madonna
lilies, lemon mint,
hyacinths, Old China

Monthly Rose,
etc., etc.
I can't see over them.

THREE BLOCKS FROM THE MOSQUE

The protestors liked to watch TV even though it always made them angry.

There were the social agitators pushing away at the edges until borders and boundaries were meaningless. Life and death; chastity and lust; this country and the next. The pro-choice activists. The militant homosexuals. Illegal immigrants. Then there were the pelicans that got some oil on their fine feathers. The protestors liked birds as much as anyone else. They would define themselves as pro-birds. Birds were good things. Their kids seemed to like them. They flew in the air quite nicely. But still. They were birds, after all.

No point in getting themselves worked up about those things. Not today anyway. They already knew what they were protesting today: the mosque to be built three blocks from the site. The holy site. The site where it all had happened. Three blocks. The protestors could remember back in the day when the foreigners understood what the word foreigner meant. It meant: away from. It meant: I will keep my distance. It meant: I know you may come to realize I'm a good person as long as I don't step foot on your land. Somehow over the years the foreigners lost a sense of who they are.

Three blocks. No way now would the protestors come to realize the foreigners were good people. They blew their chance.

Three blocks. A lot can happen in three blocks. The protestors knew that. That's what got them off the couch and into the streets. That's why after all these years they finally got cable. They didn't want to miss their favorite shows: re-runs of *I Love Lucy* and CNN.

Three blocks. So much could happen in three blocks. One of the protestors' teenage boys went astray and helped rob some liquor store. The police nabbed him after he ran three blocks. Some other protestor had a heart attack while out jogging. No one was around. For three blocks he crawled on the ground until a car stopped and helped him out. Some time ago a monsoon had swept down during a parade, and everyone was so sad. The floats drifted only three blocks before everything fell apart. It was like the whole world was contained in three blocks.

And maybe it was. Maybe the earth was flat. Then again, maybe it wasn't. Did it matter? What mattered was that it felt like the world was three blocks long. On a flat, dull surface. Ornamented with homosexuals, badly dressed activists, and self-pitying birds.

You had to move the mosque. There was no choice. The mosque was an endpoint. An endpoint is a limitation. The world shouldn't be limited to a mere three blocks. It needed to go on and on and on. It needed to stretch out far enough to circle back on itself, so the world was round and ready, ready and open to be cut and measured for appropriate boundaries.

ODE TO PROMISCUITY

From you, I need numbers, a few
simple guidelines. Numbers that tell me
how many men I need to be with
to claim I am a slut, a person
with insatiable curiosity
for everyone around me. Don't deny me
the ability to say I no longer need
one more. Look there's one
whom I saw looking back at me
in the airport terminal. Or take
the one who was so beautiful
I had no idea why
he would spend his time in the aisles
of a library following homely men
like myself. I should stop
there. But there's always one more
even when you've drawn
a limit. Or a caricature
of yourself full, bloated
with something as tasteless
as desire.

Secret Ingredients

written in collaboration with Phil E. Young

By the time she died, she'd only learned how to cook one thing. This didn't cause her any shame. Everyone loved her dish. "What's the secret ingredient?" they'd ask, and she'd tell them, and then they'd say, "Really?" and go home and try it themselves. It never turned out, no matter how many times they attempted it. Frustrated, they'd call her and ask, "We used your secret ingredient. Why didn't it work?" to which she would say, "Oh. I should have said, There are two secret ingredients. I'm not giving the second one up." But the truth was, there was no second secret ingredient. The trick was simply in combining the original ingredients in just the right way, and it could only be done by intuition, not by plan. Of course they'd all get it wrong. She took perverse pleasure imagining her friends plumbing the spice rack, racking their brains with each new bungled try. What was missing? Was it sage? Was it cinnamon? Was it (God forbid) anise? Tasting and tasting, and every taste wrong. It was none of these things. It was nothing. No one, she'd laugh to herself, thinks of nothing. But nothing was going to stand in the way of her best friend, who was determined to find out that secret ingredient, no matter what. Her best friend dropped by, e-mailed, called at all hours, first with guesses, then with pleading, finally, with threats. "Look," said her friend," if you don't tell me the ingredient, our friendship is over." Their friendship was literally going to end over nothing. And, still, for some reason, she discovered that she could not, would not, tell the truth. One night, after their children and husbands had fallen asleep, they both snuck out of their houses and met at the local park. "This is it," said her friend. It was like the climactic showdown in a spy novel. The air was so quiet outside that all you could hear was the emptiness of an ultimatum, the dumb show of refusal. Standing here, so silent for so long, the women grew tired. They called a truce and lay on their backs. With still nothing much to say, they began to admire the stars. Those dumb ornaments! Those useless things! Things that begged to be snatched from the sky, that ever-present nothingness. Why not be as shameless as they were in their kitchen, grabbing whatever they needed from their cupboards and cabinets, pretending it solved, for the time being, the answer to whatever secrets they kept just for the sake of it.

PSALM

Mental illness: a busted
Advent calendar. Time stops.

Or is skipped over. Or you're waiting
for it to begin again.

And again. Remember
no matter what

Jesus will take a number.

TSUNAMI

I can't enter the mind
      of an angry bolt of lightening. I can't
            enter the mind of desperate

whirlpool, manic
      water, no matter how much
            I may think

I want to drown. I can't enter the mind of a wave
      train. All the world seems to offer:
            how to choke and splash.

O Lord Almighty, how silly am I
      that I'd beg You for coal to shovel
            into this fiery furnace—

shelter against Your rain, against
      Your tide and Your tirade—
            against the unforgiving

world. It presents us with nothing
      except the cruel gift
            of speed. Once I saw

myself standing on railroad tracks, waiting
      for something, I suppose,
            like relief. Need I tell You?

I was not a hero. I bowed my head and let
      the gales cross through an overpass
            of unforeseen light. They knocked

me from an impending tunnel of doom.
      Why, Jesus, could you not harbor
            Your wind and Your wave

in the heavens above? I can't enter
    the wrath of Your weather
        as thousands and thousands

perish. I can't enter the mind of a God
    who coasts through our mortality
        with words as shallow

as sacrifice. I can't kneel and pray on a sea
    floor that begs me once again to mistake
        its flatness for something divine.

GET-AWAY

written in collaboration with Phil E. Young

His New Year's resolution was to give up human contact, any sort of social interaction whatsoever. He stocked up on food and water, buying it from a local survivalist camp. The people there were more than happy to leave him alone. They considerately avoided eye contact and abstained from small talk. But he found that even their polite distance and understanding was too much. It annoyed him. Even deliberate evasion is, after all, a reaction between person and person; he wanted to move beyond that, to the purity of the point on the horizon where even imaginary lines between himself and others snapped entirely, where no one acknowledged him, and he acknowledged no one. He supposed that even his decision to end all human contact was a reaction, a part in an equation, but he accepted that as one of two small sacrifices to his integrity. The other was the fact that the books he took with him, though all technical manuals and instruction guides dealing entirely with machines or building tips, were themselves written by human beings. Oh, well, no helping that... not at least until he devised his own computer algorithm that would write appropriately bland notes, directions, and algebraic propositions. To avoid the risk of a surprise visit from the federal government, he left his financial affairs in the hands of a large accounting firm (impersonal enough to not really count as human). His taxes would be deducted from his bank account automatically. Where he was going, cash was out of the question. Not only was money a symbol of exchange between humans, it had people's faces on it, for crying out loud. Goodbye, George, Abe, and Benjamin Franklin. And, of course, no talking to animals. Or plants. Even though he always refrained from anthropomorphizing his neighbor's dog who peed on his lawn from time to time or chatting up the Venus flytrap his ex-lover gave him for Christmas, he couldn't take any chances. Rules were rules. He had to be cautious about the weather. Some people cursed bad weather as if it were a naughty relative, or a pesky child. No way was he going to fall into that trap. And so it went. Being absolutely alone, he found, was incredibly hard work. Halfway to the mountain where he planned to disappear, his car began to smoke and sputter. And, wouldn't you know it, it came to a gasping halt right in the middle of a tourist area, where there were plenty of gas stations, and mechanics, and people who could help. Goddamn the luck. He was so tempted to shout aloud something obscene, but at the last second he stopped himself, afraid that there would be an echo, a voice he might want to mistake as someone else's.

A LOVE POEM FOR PHIL

Who else could make
my trips to the psych ER

feel like first dates? Afterwards
we always visited

Friendly's,
binged on hot fudge

sundaes. Two
apiece! Good thing

major depression takes
away a few pounds. Egads!

See the exclamation
marks. Those

are for you. I promise:
there's more where

those came from.

32 Down

The New York Times crossword
puzzle. 32 down: Matthew Shepard.
Parallel to Waco Texas, Abraham

Lincoln. Safety in a puzzle
everyone's figured out.
Homosexual octogenarians tack

Bible passages to their school office doors.
They shout, *David!*
Jonathan! What an item. Everyone already discovered

them eons ago. The teachers shrink away to their Fire
Island retirement home, more flames
of the same. How long does it take

for a metaphor to die? How long
can you claim a martyr is reborn
in a place as musty

as your own mind? Matthew Shepard,
blonde, blue, a hot ticket
after all this time. I pretend his name

is in a lottery: a trope scattered
round and round, where it goes
every homo knows. Here in a poem

you could claim the call-out
inevitable, the game rigged.
Does it matter when the riddle

is death, the questions always slain?

Shoelaces

*after reading in a report of the slaying of
Matthew Shepard that the murderer used
Shepard's own shoelaces to tie his feet to
the fence where he was left to die*

For at least three weeks,
I could not bring myself

to tie my own shoes.
I wore Birkenstocks,

which chafed my feet.
I did not complain.

A friend of mine expresses
her joy over having kids

as often as I think about
you, Matthew. In other words:

a bit too habitually. She means
well. As I do. This is not

what I should wonder: why did
they take the time to remove

your shoes? Did the clean-up
workers (Are there even such people?)

rip the laces in one bold stroke
or did someone take the time

to unlace them as carefully
as you would a Christmas present?

I am in a childless relationship
with a man who has infinite

patience for my temper tantrums
and overall bratty ways.

Once he met my friend,
arm-wrestled her children.

He did not let them win. I loved
him for that. Later he shared

our private dream: basking
in the happiness of tying

your son's shoes
on the first day of school,

knowing that he will march
into the world safe and protected

by a gesture
you always take for granted.

ODE TO MY LOVER

Don't forgive me
for laughing

when you confessed
months after Matthew

Shepard died
that you yourself

had once been gay-
bashed in the back

parking lot
of a 7-Eleven. It didn't

seem like that big
of a deal. No

permanent injuries.
You told the story

right after we made
love so it felt

like an excuse
to make me

hold you a bit
longer when I wanted

to go to bed, or find
someone else

on the Internet. Did you
ever think of Matthew

when I was
sucking your cock,

not being very careful
with my teeth? I am

not always nice. Once
I cheated on you

with a trick
who was pretty

much forgettable
except for his porn

stash I "accidentally"
found: he cut out

a photo of Aaron
McKinney and taped

his head on the body
of a limp muscle

model. That slut always
wanted things rougher.

"Can't," I said. "I save
that kind of stuff

for my boyfriend." He never
looked angry. Just

docile, needy. A victim
too weak

to hurt.

ODE TO JUDY
SHEPARD

I imagine
your pain
after
you give
a speech
to a college audience.
You watch
someone
in the front row
applaud,
determined
to show
his respect
for you.
You want
him
to stop.
Gratitude
can be
the most
difficult thing
to enjoy.
But you
always end
up pitying
the man
who is scared
to stop
clapping.
His hands
grow
so red,
they look
almost
sunburned,
as if left
in a field,

unguarded
from the
outside
weather and
whatever else
is there.

ODE TO MATTHEW SHEPARD

Once I hit
someone I loved.

It wasn't
very hard. But

I hit him. I
hit him

the way you
hit someone

you need
to stop

loving you. I
can still

remember the way
the body looked

when I hit it.
It was ruined

with my knowing
you could hurt

a body and it
still needs

something
more than

your pain.
Narrative is

as corrupt
as the thoughts

of the men who
murdered

you, Matthew.
Explanation never

satisfies. It
always wants

something
like redemption.

ODE TO MATTHEW SHEPARD

I see one of my students at the end of the bar and want to say:
    Matthew Shepard, what are you doing here? It's a school night.
But his name isn't Matthew. And it's not a school night.
    It is Saturday. I am here at the Hole in the Wall alone.
Forty years old. Twice the age that you, Matthew, were
    before you died. You can see the lines under my eyes,
the gray in my hair, my flabby belly. Here I like to pretend
    that everyone is looking at me. I pretend a lot of things.
Take that guy in the corner with the big, blue eyes.
    He is a Silver Fox. I imagine him taking me out
to his pick-up truck, ordering me to drop to my knees. After we're done,
    he says, "You're not all that bad." I am touched.
For now, I sit here, watching my student at the end of the bar.
    I can't remember his name—I can't remember any of their names.
I never keep office hours. I never grade papers. I never make a lesson plan.
    Go home. Get a head start on your homework, I want to say.
How did I receive a B+ in my undergrad Gay and Lesbian Lit course?
    This question haunts me more
than the recent deaths of young gay men. I can still remember
    my lit teacher's all black wardrobe. He joked: "I'm the only gay man
who wants to look like Johnny Cash." On the first day of class,
    he told us: "Don't take notes. All that's important
is you find a date." My dumb friend received a solid A.
    "It takes a full hour and someone else's credit card
to look this good," he said. "I deserve that grade." A decade later,
    someone sent me the teacher's mug shot from the newspaper.
Arrested for crystal meth. Served him right. Now here I am in this bar,
    tapping the shoulder of the unattractive man
next to me and asking, "Which guy here do you think most wants to fall
    to their knees?" My undergrad years: frequenting the Fruit Loop
where men in cars drove in circles. Once a man pulled over and asked me to take
    his hand, escorting me behind the tallest trees.
He said right before he went down, "Allow desperation
    to be your teacher." I had no idea what he was talking about.
I still don't. All I remember is the stupid wind through the leaves.
    All I know is you, Matthew, are dead,
my student is sitting at the end of the bar, and I need one last drink.

Once during a conference, I had a student who broke
out in hives. He began scratching and scratching.
    "Would you mind scratching, too?" he said and lifted up
his shirt. There were dozens of small red welts. He guided my hand
        to his back. Once he let go, I scratched. This was sex.
This was love. This was the happy ending: He dropped my class.
    Here in this bar my student pretends
not to see me. He will not look in my direction. It makes me want to hold him
        down and say: *Don't leave this bar.*
You never know what could happen to you. This is what it means
        to be a homosexual: People want you dead. Maybe even a teacher
at the other end of the bar.
    Matthew, O Matthew, you died in a field. Is an elegy anything
other than a taunt? A way of saying: *Look at me. I'm still alive.*
    Is an elegy anything other than a compliment to oneself? A way of saying:
I'm special for recognizing you're special. Is an elegy anything
        other than saying: *Free drinks on me!* A way of saying: One last round.

ODE TO MATTHEW
SHEPARD

I had never expected
to hear a writer talk

about people who died
from the 1918 influenza

pandemic with such relish.
She imagined

the suffering of victims
so vividly

everyone gave her personae
poems awards.

In a conference, I asked
her: *How worried were you*

about hurting the dead?
Was it ethical to make

their ghosts relive the pain?
She looked

right through me,
as if I was dead.

"The dead owe me,"
she said. "I brought them

back to life.
I am their God."

She then rattled
off a few kind things

about my poems,
and asked if I could send in

the next writer.
I promise, Matthew,

I will never speak
for you. Only, I hope,

near you.

UPON IMAGINING THE FIELD WHERE MATTHEW SHEPARD WAS MURDERED

Beyond the field
is another young gay man. This one

lurks in chatrooms
to steal money from lonely

mothers whose sons have died
of AIDS. Beyond the field

is a mother who buys her living
gay son a Chippendales calendar

for Christmas and then gets angry
when he doesn't seem grateful. Beyond

the field are people still thankful
that a faggot got what he deserved.

Beyond the field is a gay man
who boasts that he never

watches porn. Beyond the field
is a gay man who thinks

he's a rebel because he doesn't
shave his balls. Beyond the field

is a gay man who calls uncircumcised
penises "pigs

in a blanket." Beyond the field
is a gay man who is more sexist

than any straight guy. He always
has to befriend the most attractive

straight woman to show the world
everyone wants him.

Beyond the field is someone
who saw *Forrest Gump* twice

and was convinced that was the movie
Tom Hanks plays a homosexual.

Beyond the field is a gay man
who wants to be beaten to death

by someone's bare hands
so that someone will finally touch him.

Beyond the field is an openly gay man
who claims his meth addiction

was caused by "society's oppression
of homosexuals." Even his lesbian

psychiatrist
won't let him get away

with that one. Beyond the field is a president
who won't allow

for gay marriage, but treats
an old transsexual friend with complete

respect. Beyond the field are porn
tapes of bareback sex hidden in the toolshed.

They are found by a wife
who will be relieved

the day he confesses. She wants to inform
him about the beauty

of condoms. As he did
with their children. Beyond

the field is the fact the universe cannot
keep secrets. Beyond the field

is a gay group
of graduate students who asked someone

not to reveal
he was gay-bashed.

They don't want the story to bring
down everyone's morale.

Beyond the field is the fat
body of a gay man

who purges his lunch
in the toilet after another trick

neglects to call him. Beyond
the field is that same trick

ironing the creases
of his favorite shirt

so that when he goes to the gay bar
the man he loves will finally

love him back. Beyond the field are happy
endings not created

by synthetic compounds. Beyond
the field is a God

who is bored
with rainbow

necklaces. Beyond the field
is me who begs forgiveness

for his own self-
inflated ego. These simple words

that no one else needs
except me. Beyond the field

is a student disowned
by his family and deluded.

As I once was. He wants
and wants. For the words

to bring
what he never had

back. He does not need to know
yet

that the world shares his wish. Why
be cruel and tell him

he's nothing
special? Beyond the field is field.

Beyond the field. Beyond.

About the Author

Steve Fellner is the author of *The Weary World Rejoices* (Marsh Hawk Press, 2011), a memoir, *All Screwed Up* (Benu Press, 2009), and *Blind Date with Cavafy* (Marsh Hawk Press, 2007). *Blind Date with Cavafy* won the Thom Gunn Gay Male Poetry Award. He currently teaches at SUNY Brockport and lives with his husband Phil E. Young.

Titles From Marsh Hawk Press

Steve Fellner, *The Weary World Rejoices*
Mary Mackey, *Sugar Zone*
Stephen Paul Miller, *There's Only One God and You're Not It*
Thomas Fink, *Peace Conference*
Justin Petropoulos, *Eminent Domain*
Daniel Morris, *If Not for the Courage*
Norman Finkelstein, *Inside the Ghost Factory*
Neil de la Flor, *Almost Dorothy*
Phillip Lopate, *At the End of the Day: Selected Poems and An Introductory Essay*
Sandy McIntosh, *Ernesta, in the Style of the Flamenco*
Eileen Tabios, *The Thorn Rosary: Selected Prose Poems and New (1998–2010)*
Paul Pines, *Last Call at the Tin Palace*
Corrine Robins, *Facing It: New and Selected Poems*
Edward Foster, *The Beginning of Sorrows.*
Stephen Paul Miller, *Fort Dad*
Patricia Carlin, *Quantum Jitters*
Michael Rerick, *In Ways Impossible to Fold*
Harriet Zinnes, *Light Light or the Curvature of the Earth*
Rochelle Ratner, *Ben Casey Days*
Jane Augustine, *A Woman's Guide to Mountain Climbing*
Thomas Fink, *Clarity and Other Poems*
Karin Randolph, *Either She Was*
Norman Finkelstein, *Passing Over*
Sandy McIntosh, *Forty-Nine Guaranteed Ways to Escape Death*
Eileen Tabios, *The Light Sang As It Left Your Eyes*
Claudia Carlson, *The Elephant House*
Steve Fellner, *Blind Date with Cavafy*

Basil King, *77 Beasts: Basil King's Bestiary*
Rochelle Ratner, *Balancing Acts*
Corinne Robins, *Today's Menu*
Mary Mackey, *Breaking the Fever*
Sigman Byrd, *Under the Wanderer's Star*
Edward Foster, *What He Ought To Know*
Sharon Olinka, *The Good City*
Harriet Zinnes, *Whither Nonstopping*
Sandy McIntosh, *The After-Death History of My Mother*
Eileen R. Tabios, *I Take Thee, English, for My Beloved*
Burt Kimmelman, *Somehow*
Stephen Paul Miller, *Skinny Eighth Avenue*
Jacquelyn Pope, *Watermark*
Jane Augustine, *Night Lights*
Thomas Fink, *After Taxes*
Martha King, *Imperfect Fit*
Susan Terris, *Natural Defenses*
Daniel Morris, *Bryce Passage*
Corinne Robins, *One Thousand Years*
Chard deNiord, *Sharp Golden Thorn*
Rochelle Ratner, *House and Home*
Basil King, *Mirage*
Sharon Dolin, *Serious Pink*
Madeline Tiger, *Birds of Sorrow and Joy*
Patricia Carlin, *Original Green*
Stephen Paul Miller, *The Bee Flies in May*
Edward Foster, *Mahrem: Things Men Should Do for Men*
Eileen R. Tabios, *Reproductions of the Empty Flagpole*
Harriet Zinnes, *Drawing on the Wall*
Thomas Fink, *Gossip: A Book of Poems*
Jane Augustine, *Arbor Vitae*
Sandy McIntosh, *Between Earth and Sky*
Burt Kimmelman and Fred Caruso, *The Pond at Cape May Point*